Paper Punching

Julie Taylor

ISBN Number: 978-1-907267-01-7

First published in Great Britain 2009

masterCRAFT
Magmaker Ltd
Cromwell Court, New Road,
St Ives, Cambs PE27 5BF, UK

Text and photographs © Magmaker Limited

ISBN Number: 978-1-907267-01-7

Published by: Magmaker Ltd, Cromwell Court,
                     New Road, St Ives, Cambs PE27 5BF, UK
                     t: 01480 496130
                     f: 01480 495514
                     w: www.magmaker.co.uk
Author: Julie Taylor
Editor: Peter Law
                     e: peter.law@magmaker.co.uk
Design: Lucy Kirkman, RMG Design + Print Ltd
                     w: www.rmgpublishing.co.uk
Photography: Brett Caines
Publishing director: Peter Raven

Stocked by most good craft shops or available at £4.95 plus p&p
from e: mastercraft@magmaker.co.uk

Contents

Introduction   page 8
Materials & equipment   page 10
Preparation & punch care   page 12
Basic techniques   page 15
Butterflies card   page 16
Simple floral card   page 19
Black and silver gift card   page 22
Bookmark   page 25
Pillow gift box   page 28
Bold floral greetings card   page 33
Decorated photo frame   page 37
Hearts and lace trinket box   page 40
Retro notebook cover   page 44
Dinner party table setting decorations   page 48
Hanging floral wreath   page 53
Potted plant   page 57
Cherry blossom necklace   page 62
Masculine leaves card   page 66
Scrapbook-style wall-mounted picture   page 70
3D floral greetings card   page 74
Gardener's concertina notebook   page 78

Introduction

Craft punches are simply more elaborate versions of the office hole punch. As their usefulness and versatility for paper crafters have become apparent the punches have become more elaborate in the shapes that they punch and better designed for craft purposes. You can now purchase punches that decorate corners, punch borders, emboss at the same time as cut, and ones that you squeeze rather than depress. With so many wonderful punches now available you may wonder where to start with your purchases.

As with many items, sometimes the simplest designs are the most versatile. I find that I use my basic corner rounder, a few trusty flower punches, and basic circle and heart punches the most. More specialised shapes such as paw prints, teddy bears and witches have their uses for specific projects, but do not make it to my Top Ten list or to those that I would like with me on a desert island.

Paper punches may have originated as an office supply, but don't let that lead you into thinking that what you can create with them is limited and uninspiring. A little simple decoration or folding transforms the basic punched shape into a work of art.

Most people who enjoy making cards will have a few punches, but their use is not restricted to card-making. They are equally useful for scrapbooking and all paper crafts. I have used them for mixed media projects and jewellery-making and as stencils for textile projects. In this book you will be shown step-by-step how to make 3D flowers in a pot,

"I have used punches for mixed media projects and jewellery-making and as stencils for textile projects."

design a necklace, create a wall art, decorate a trinket box and make a floral wreath as well as many other projects – all with a few craft punches.

The projects in this book take you step-by-step through the techniques you need to get the most out of the punches you buy, starting with the most basic punching for absolute beginners through to advanced projects using multiple techniques. All the projects use readily available materials and can be adapted for alternative punches should you not wish to buy the ones used in the specific projects.

I've thoroughly enjoyed creating the projects and I hope that whether you're a beginner making your first punch purchase or an 'old-hand' whose punches may have been relegated to the back of a drawer you find inspiration in these pages to get creative and enjoy the simple pleasures of punching.

Julie Taylor

Materials & equipment

Paper punches are essentially two pieces of metal that, when you depress the punch with the paper inside, slide together cutting through the paper, just as the blades of a pair of scissors slide together.

Punches come in an ever-increasing variety of forms. The original punches were all **button punches**. You press down on the centre button to make it cut. Many of these are now being replaced with **lever punches**, which require less force to operate. If you have weak or arthritic hands, try to choose a lever type. If you have a button punch and are struggling, try placing it upside down and use both hands, one on top of the other.

Long arm punches allow you to punch your shape further away from the edge of the paper. They're useful for creating small apertures in cards. **Plier punches** are extremely useful as they are easy to use and will cut through a wider variety of materials but are available only in a few designs. **Squeeze punches** are relatively new to the market, again, are easier to use, and will often take thicker card, but are also limited in the choice of designs.

Corner punches do exactly as their name suggests (although I do show you in one project how to use them for another purpose). The variety of designs available has snowballed over recent years. **Border punches** cut a decorative edge to your paper and once again the number of designs available has flourished.

Punch and emboss punches are probably the most recent addition to the market. They are ideal for making paper flowers, but cut only thin paper.

A **punch aid** is useful if you find button punches difficult to operate. You place the punch and paper inside and press down on the lever, providing more force than you can give with your thumb alone.

Items useful for decorating your punched shapes include fine-line pens, inkpads, decorating chalks, glitter, brads and eyelets, small buttons and adhesive gems.

You'll also need basic equipment such as plenty of paper and card, pencil, ruler, paper cutter, tweezers to help place small punched shapes, and double-sided and 3D foam tape.

Other items of equipment used in the projects include blank MDF (medium density fibre board) or papier mâché boxes and photo frames, polystyrene wreath, Vilene, air drying clay, ribbon and wire. Punches are available from the following stockists: Woodware, Craftime and Trimcraft.

button punch

lever punch

long arm punch

plier punch

squeeze punch

corner punch

border punch

punch & emboss

punch aid

11

Preparation & punch care

Your punches should last you a lifetime if they are properly looked after and stored carefully.

Punches are designed only to cut paper and thin card. Punches are normally very robust, but the surest way to break one is to try cutting card that is too thick for it to manage. The basic rule of thumb is the more elaborate the punch, the thinner the paper it will accept. If you find your punch resisting, do not force it, but try a thinner material.

Other materials that you can punch are vellum and metal shim. Vilene is a non-woven fabric and can be cut using small, simple punch shapes. Other materials that are half-way between paper and fabric can also often be cut. If they have a fairly open weave, try placing on a sheet of paper before cutting. Adhesive paper can also be cut, but do so sparingly or the punch mechanism will clog with glue.

Just like scissors, your punches can go blunt. To keep them sharp, punch several times over through some very fine sandpaper or tin foil. If your punch is sticking it can be lubricated by punching through wax paper.

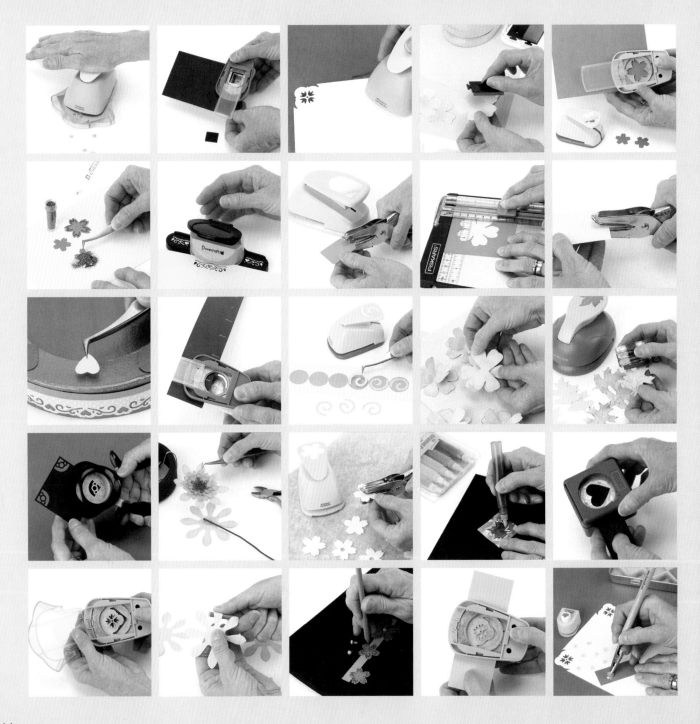

Basic techniques

The basic punching technique is extremely simple. Slide the paper that you wish to cut into the punch and depress the button or lever, release the mechanism, allow the punched shape to fall out and remove the paper. When you're pressing down on your punch you'll find it easiest to do so on a firm work surface.

This technique is fine, but if like most crafters you are frugal with your paper, or you simply wish to see exactly where you're punching, it's best to use your punch upside down.

If it's a button punch place it upside down on a table, slide in the paper and press down on the punch with the palm of your hand. If it's a lever punch, slide the paper in and hold firm with one hand and squeeze the punch with the other.

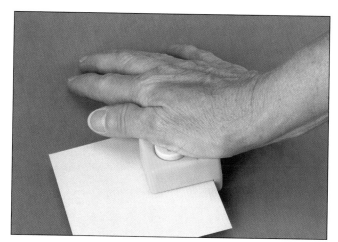

Technique for button punch

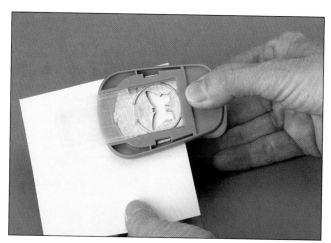

Technique for lever punch

Butterflies card

This is an ideal starter project on which to practise punching as you need only two punches.

The various shades of one or two colours make this card effective.

A good way to get lots of different shades of a single colour is to punch the shapes from pictures in an old magazine. It doesn't matter whether the paper is patterned or plain, but resist the temptation to introduce more colours. Use the larger punch for darker shades and the smaller punch for the lighter tones. By placing mainly large dark-coloured butterflies in the centre and the smaller lighter-coloured ones towards the corners, the central ones appear to be closer, with the smaller ones flying in to the distance.

You can make different versions of this card by varying the paper colours. You could also replace the butterfly punches with dragonflies, hearts, flowers or stars.

Why not try the same design on a different shape card blank?

You will need:

- Butterfly punch in two sizes
- 15cm square white card blank
- 14.5cm square of dark pink card
- 14cm square of plain white card
- A wide variety of pink and purple coloured paper
- Glue

Step by Step Instructions

① Punch lots of butterflies from your coloured papers. Hold the punch upside down so you can see exactly where you're punching.

② Cut a 14cm square of plain white card and glue centrally to a 14.5cm square of pink card.

③ Mount onto the front of your card blank.

④ Arrange the butterflies on top, putting the darker ones in towards the centre of the card and the smaller lighter coloured ones towards the top and bottom corners.

⑤ Lift one butterfly at a time and glue in place by the centre of its body only.

⑥ When the glue is dry bend the wings up a little to give a 3D effect.

Hints & Tips Punch more butterflies than you actually need so that you can experiment with colours and positioning.

Simple floral card

In this project you learn how to make the best use of a few punches by combining simple punched shapes to make more detailed focal points for your crafting.

You'll soon find that by making small changes to the designs you get very different looks. Varying the colour of the flowers and the background will create variety. Pick colours that you know the recipient likes or tends to wear a lot. Try monochromatic or black and white designs. Use the same design but with different-shaped flower punches or heart or leaf punches. Try rotating the squares so that they become diamonds.

| **Hints & Tips** | You can vary the size of the card blank. It's not crucial to the project. |

You will need:

- Cherry blossom punch in three sizes (3.5cm, 2.5cm and 1.5cm)
- Small hole punch
- Scalloped (3.5cm) square punch (5cm across diagonal)
- Small (1.5cm) square punch (2.5cm across diagonal)
- 17.5cm x 7.5cm cream card blank
- Thin cream, pink and green card
- 3D foam tape
- Glue

Step by Step Instructions

1. Cut a 15cm x 6cm rectangle of pink card and attach centrally to the card blank.

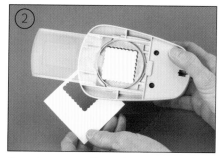

2. Punch one scalloped square and three small squares from cream card.

3. Punch one large flower from pink card, one medium flower from green card and four small flowers from pink card.

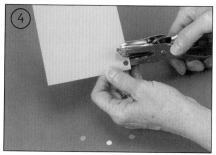

4. Punch one cream and four green small circles from a hole punch, collecting them as they fall.

5. Glue the three sizes of flower on top of each other in descending order of size with a cream circle in the middle.

6. Attach the finished flower to the centre of the scalloped square.

7. Attach the square towards the top of the pink rectangle with 3D foam tape.

8. Glue the remaining small pink flowers to the small cream squares and glue a green circle to the centre of each.

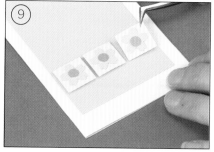

9. Attach these three squares towards the bottom of the card with 3D foam tape.

Black and silver gift card

Corner punches can be either simple affairs that literally round a corner on a piece of paper or ones that create a punched design in the corner as well as creating a curved or patterned edge to the corner. They are a very useful addition to your craft box and are likely to be used time and time again.

We will use both types of corner punch in this project. The simple corner rounder creates the curves on the outside edges of the gift card. The ornate corner punch creates the pretty pattern for the main design. The waste that falls from the punch is used on the diamond in the centre.

You could make the same project on a larger scale to create a greetings card rather than a gift card. You could also decorate the inside edge of the card with some of the punched waste pieces.

You will need:

- Simple corner rounder punch
- Ornate corner punch
- Small (1.5cm) square punch (2.5cm across diagonal)
- Small hole punch
- Thin black card
- Silver paper or thin card
- Silver thread
- 3D foam tape
- Glue

Step by Step Instructions

Cut a 7cm x 14cm rectangle of thin black card. Fold in half to create a 7cm square gift card.

Use the simple corner rounder to create a curve on each of the four corners of the gift card, front and back.

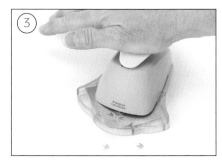

Cut a 6cm square of silver paper and punch each corner in turn with the ornate punch. Retain some of the punched waste pieces.

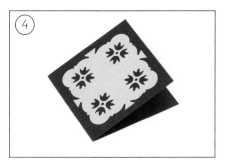

Glue the design to the front of the gift card.

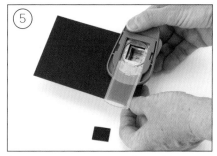

Punch a small square from black card.

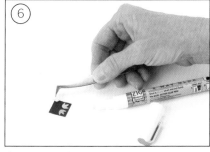

Glue one of the retained waste pieces in each corner.

Attach to the front of the design with 3D foam tape.

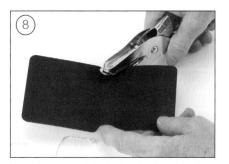

Punch a small hole in the back of the gift card and loop a length of silver thread through to create a tie.

Hints & Tips Corner punches usually have a guide on the back— make sure that both edges of the paper are flush against it when you punch.

Bookmark

Punched shapes are a great way to make repeat patterns. They can range from simple and elegant to intricate and complicated simply by rotating, flipping and layering the shapes.

The simplest of punched shapes make the best patterns. You will soon find that there are dozens of variations that you can make using just three or four punches. If you want to flip shapes make sure you use paper or thin card that is coloured on both sides. Your patterns will have many uses. Try making gift cards and greetings cards using the same technique.

You will need:

- 2.5cm circle punch
- 2.5cm spiral punch
- 1cm heart punch
- 1cm sun punch
- Small hole punch
- 17cm x 5cm rectangle of cream card for the bookmark
- Glue
- Tweezers
- Turquoise, yellow, pink and purple paper
- Turquoise, yellow and purple embroidery cotton

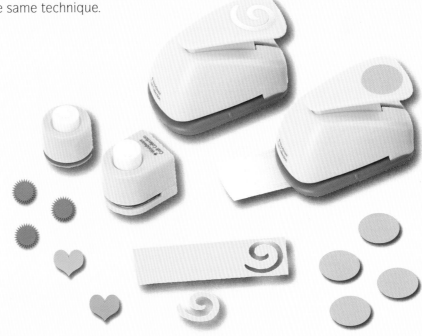

Step by Step Instructions

Punch a hole at the base of the bookmark.

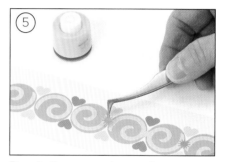

Punch six circles from turquoise paper. Place them next to one another in a line down the centre of the bookmark. Glue them in place.

Punch six spirals from yellow paper. Glue the spirals on top of the circles, rotating every alternate one through 180 degrees.

Punch six hearts from pink paper and four from purple. Place in the valleys between the circles, alternating the colours. Glue in place.

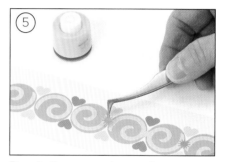

Punch three sun shapes from purple paper and two from pink. Place at the points where the turquoise circles join, alternating the colours as you go.

Hints & Tips Use tweezers to put the smaller shapes in position.

Cut three 20cm lengths of embroidery cotton in purple, yellow and turquoise. Place the strands together and fold in half.

Push the folded end through the hole in the base of the bookmark and pull the ends through the loop to form a tassel.

Pillow gift box

In previous projects we've used the shapes just as they come out of the punch. In this project we make the shapes more detailed by decorating them before use.

Punched shapes can be decorated in a wide variety of ways. You can add glitter, adhesive gems, peel-off stickers, brads or eyelets.

You don't need to be an artist to add simple pen markings such as veins on a leaf or single line or dashed borders around regular shapes such as a star.

Applying craft chalk to the outer edge of a shape, or swiping the edges lightly with an inkpad adds depth to the look of the shape.

Try adding small peel-off stickers to the centres of flowers or decorate the edge of a punched tag with a peel-off border.

In this project we will use a fine tip glue pen and glitter to add outlines to our punched shapes. Brads are also used to decorate the flower centres.

Step by Step Instructions

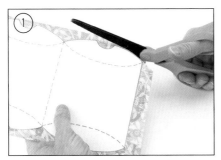

Use the template provided (on page 32) to cut a pillow gift box from turquoise card.

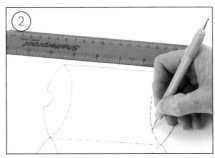

With the template still in place, use an embossing tool to score along the dotted lines. Remove the template and fold.

Glue the flap to the opposite side and fold the other edges inwards to close.

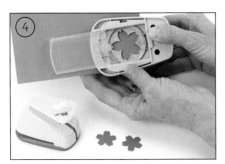

Punch one large and two small cherry blossom shapes from turquoise card.

With a glue pen draw a pattern that follows the outline on each petal. Sprinkle pink glitter over the flowers and shake off the excess.

Cut a 1cm wide strip of pink card. Attach the three cherry blossom shapes to the strip with brads.

Glue the strip to the pillow box and trim the ends.

Punch a tag from pink card. Punch a small hole in the top.

Hints & Tips You could make a larger version of the pillow box instead of an envelope for a three-dimensional card.

With a glue pen draw a 'dot-dash' line around the tag. Sprinkle turquoise glitter over the tag and shake off the excess.

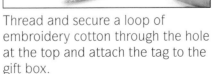

Thread and secure a loop of embroidery cotton through the hole at the top and attach the tag to the gift box.

Pattern

Cutting line
_____

Fold line
- - - - - - - - - - - - - - -

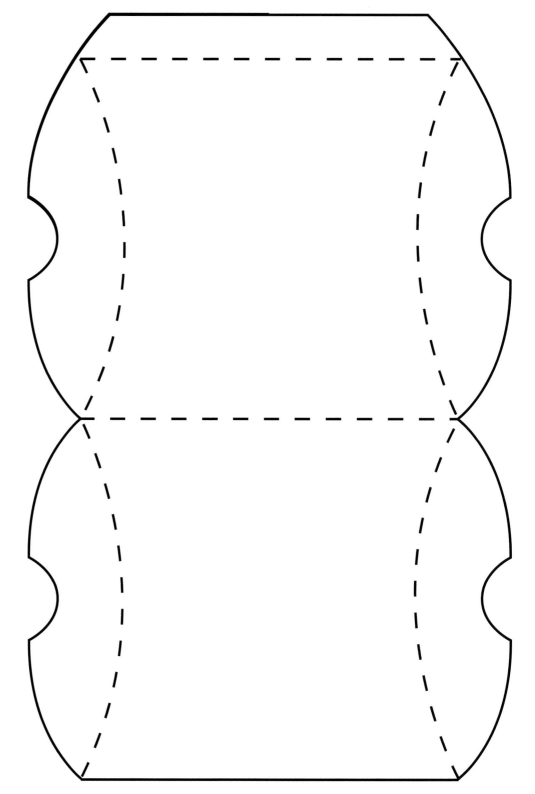

Bold floral greetings card

You'll probably have realised by now that when you're punching, the piece that is left behind, the negative space, is interesting too – far too good to be thrown to waste.

This card shows you one simple way to use those pieces. There are many others – try placing patterned paper, glitter paper, a stamped design or message behind the negative space.

Punch shapes from the front of a card blank and glue them to the corresponding position on the inside of the card.

Long reach punches are useful for this technique as you can punch the shape from the centre of the card rather than the edge.

You will need:

- 5cm cherry blossom punch
- 1.5cm daisy punch
- Thin card in green, purple and pink
- Small adhesive gem
- Pink ribbon bow
- 3D foam tape
- Glue

Step by Step Instructions

1. Cut a 14.5cm x 21cm rectangle of green card and fold in half to create a 14.5cm x 10.5cm card blank.

2. Use the small daisy punch to punch four daisies along the base of the front of the card. Reserve three of the daisies.

3. Punch a large cherry blossom from pink card. Discard the punched shape and keep the original piece that it was punched from.

4. Trim the sides so that there's an even border around the floral-shaped space.

5. Cut a piece of purple card that is slightly larger than the pink.

6. Attach the pink card with the floral aperture to the purple card using 3D foam tape.

continued over

continued

Hints & Tips Collect useable pieces of punched waste each time you craft and store in a container ready for a rainy day.

Attach to the front of the card. Glue three of the reserved green daisies to the base of the pink card.

Punch four small daisies from pink card. Glue three of them in the spaces between the punched daisies on the lower edge of the card.

Glue one in the centre of the large flower created by the negative space and add a small gem to its centre.

Glue a small pink ribbon bow between the two rows of daisies.

Decorated photo frame

Although paper punches will normally only punch thin card, by gluing two together we can make more rigid shapes which in turn can be used to create texture or 'faux embossing' on various items such as picture frames.

Blank picture frames for decorating can be bought in most general craft stores. Alternatively you could recycle an existing frame.

This particular frame has curved sides so the hearts stand away from the curve. If your frame has flat sides the hearts will be fully attached but will still provide interesting texture to the frame.

You will need:

- 2cm heart punch
- 1.5cm heart punch
- Thin card
- PVA glue
- 15.5cm x 10.5cm blank MDF (medium density fibre board) or papier mâché picture frame
- Acrylic paint

Step by Step Instructions

Punch 16 of each size heart. Glue together in twos to create eight large and eight small hearts.

Glue the hearts evenly around the picture frame. (If your frame is a different size you may wish to use more or fewer hearts.)

Hints & Tips Change the shape of the punch to suit the photo – a flower or leaf shape for a scene, a circle or diamond punch shape for a male photo.

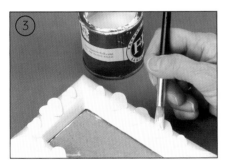

Paint the frame. If your frame is curved make sure you paint the back of the hearts – they will be seen from the side.

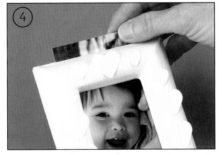

Trim your chosen photo to size and place in the frame.

Hearts and lace trinket box

Border punches have an elongated repeat design and usually cut the edge off your paper creating a decorative perforated pattern.

Most border punches have an alignment facility on either side of the punching mechanism so that you can extend the design along the entire length of your paper.

In this project we create narrow strips of paper that have a border punch design along one edge and attach them to the trinket box as 'faux lace'.

Border punches make beautiful embellished borders for greetings cards, or by punching all four sides of a square or rectangle you can make a decorative edge to a card topper.

You will need:

- MDF (medium density fibre board) or papier mâché trinket box
- Acrylic paints in blue and green
- Hearts border punch
- 7cm daisy punch
- 5cm daisy punch
- 2.5cm daisy punch
- 2cm heart punch
- 1cm heart punch
- 3D foam tape
- Blue patterned paper
- Thin card in green, light blue and dark blue
- Small pale blue adhesive gems

Step by Step Instructions

Paint your trinket box with acrylic paints. Our lid was painted in two colours but you could use just one.

Take a sheet of blue patterned paper and place the long edge in the border punch. Punch once and remove.

Place the paper back in the punch aligning the previously punched section over the printed pattern on the punch. Punch again and remove the paper.

Punch the whole length of the paper in this way. The outer straight edge should fall cleanly away leaving a pretty lacelike pattern.

Trim the paper so that the paper lace is just 1.5cm wide. You'll probably need two strips of lace to fit around your box.

Attach the paper lace approximately 2cm above the base of the box.

Cut a 0.5cm wide strip of thin green card (again, you'll probably need two) and attach to the base of the lace.

Cut more paper lace and attach around the lid of the box.

Cut a 0.5cm wide strip of thin blue card and attach to the edge of the lace.

Punch three daisies – one of each size – from pale blue card.

Attach one above the other using 3D foam tape between each layer. Glue to the centre of the lid.

Punch four 2cm hearts from dark blue card and four 1cm hearts from light blue card.

Attach alternately around the edge of the lid.

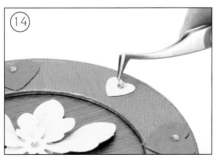

Add an adhesive gem to each heart.

Hints & Tips Only use paper in border punches – the designs are too intricate to cut card.

Retro notebook cover

We've now used single shape punches and border punches, but you can also make borders using single shape punches. The key to success is just to take a little time to measure and plan your pattern.

In this project basic punches provide the pattern to decorate a removable book cover. Use it to jazz up a boring notebook, to hide the identity of the book you're reading – or the Sudoku that you're addicted to!

You could use a similar border on a card or make the book cover on a smaller scale as a wallet to hold tickets or coupons.

Once you have completed this project you can start creating borders with other punches that you already have in your craft box. Experiment with them first by roughly punching the edge of a scrap piece of paper. Once you find a pattern you like, repeat the process, measuring and marking the distances between the punching, so that you create an even pattern.

You will need:

- Two sheets of 12in x 12in (30cm x 30cm) thin yellow card
- Thin dark brown card
- Thin beige card
- 2.5cm circle punch
- 2.5cm square punch (measured across the diagonal)
- 5cm scalloped square punch (measured across the diagonal)
- 1.5cm leaf punch
- Glue
- 3mm wide double-sided tape

Step by Step Instructions

1 Cut two pieces of yellow card 1cm taller and 5cm wider than the book you wish to cover.

2 Score and fold 5cm in from the right-hand side on one piece and 5cm in from the left-hand side of the other.

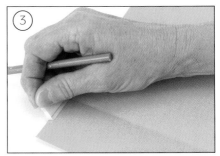

3 Attach the flaps to the inside of the covers. Place the tape right at the edges or your book will not fit inside.

4 Cut a 22cm x 4cm strip of dark brown card. Score and fold in half lengthways to create a spine for your book cover.

5 Place the front cover on top of the back cover and glue the spine to each. Check that your book fits inside.

6 Cut a 4cm wide strip of brown card, longer than the height of your book, and mark the mid-point on the underside.

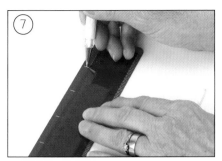

Mark and draw lines every 3cm either side of the mid-line.

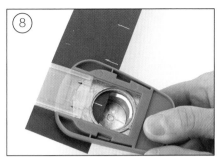

Turn your circle punch upside down and line up the arrow on the back of the punch with one of your pencil lines.

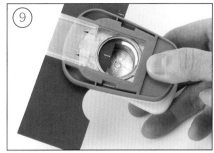

Pull the paper back slightly so that just a semi circle will be cut and punch. Move along to the next pencil line and repeat.

Continue punching in this way until you have completed one edge of the border.

Turn the strip round and repeat on the other side. Reserve three of the punched arcs for later.

Trim your pattern evenly to 21cm and attach to the book cover.

Punch seven circles from yellow card, seven small squares from beige card and seven leaves from brown card and glue to the pattern strip.

Punch three scalloped squares from beige card. Glue a brown arc to each. Attach the squares to the front cover.

Hints & Tips If you're covering a thick book, adjust the width of the spine and create two creases along it instead of one.

Dinner party table setting decorations

Many corner punches create a pattern which is ideal for folding into a three-dimensional shape.

Now we'll create some of these shapes to decorate the dining table for a special occasion. You could change the colours to match the rest of your tableware.

The project consists of one napkin ring, one place card and one menu card. Just repeat the instructions to make as many settings as you need.

You could also use the same designs on the invitations and add them to favour boxes, or simply glue one to the top of each after-dinner mint!

Your dinner party will be remembered as much for the paper crafting as the meal.

If you replace the floral centre with heart-shaped ones the projects would be ideal for a wedding breakfast table.

You will need:

- Thin white card
- Thin black card
- Corner squeeze punch – pearls design
- 1cm flower punch
- Scoring tool
- Small silver brads
- 3mm double-sided tape

Step by Step Instructions

For place card. Fold a 6cm x 10cm rectangle of white card in half to make a 3 x 10cm place card. Glue a 3mm wide strip of black card to the lower edge.

Cut one 3.5cm square of black card and one of white card. Punch all corners of both squares with the pearls design corner punch.

Take the punched white square and carefully fold each corner forward to the centre of the square. Glue on top of the black square.

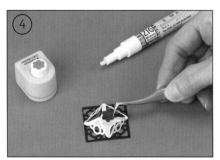

Punch a small flower from black card and glue to the inside centre of the design. Allow the folded edges to lie slightly raised.

Mount on a 4cm square of white card and attach to the place card.

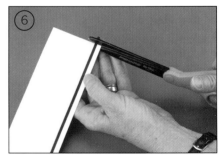

For napkin ring. Cut a 6cm x 15cm rectangle of white card. Attach a 3mm wide strip of black card about 0.5cm above the base. Trim to fit.

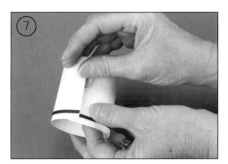

Roll the card into a tube, overlap and glue the ends to make the napkin ring.

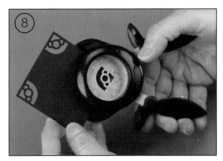

Cut a 6cm square of black card. Punch all corners with the pearls design corner punch.

Mark the mid-point along each straight edge of the square. Use a scoring tool to score a line between adjacent mid-points.

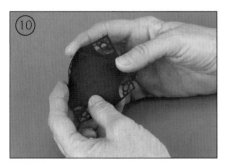

Fold the corners inwards along these scored lines.

Fold outwards again at the same point as you folded on the place card.

Cut a 3.5cm square of white card. Punch each corner and attach to the inside of the folded black square.

Hints & Tips Try using an alternative corner punch – the pattern will be different, but just as much fun.

continued over

continued

Attach a punched black flower to the centre of the design with a silver brad and secure the design to the napkin ring.

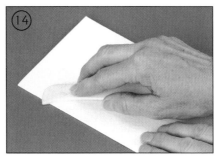

For menu card. Cut a 21cm square of white card. Score and fold in half to make a 21cm x 10.5cm card.

Cut a 3mm wide strip of black card and attach about 1cm away from the fold. Trim to fit.

Create the same motif that was used for the napkin holder and attach to the centre of the card.

Create two unmounted place card motifs and attach them to the menu card, above and below the central design.

Print your menu and attach to the inside.

Hanging floral wreath

Some punches will both cut a shape and emboss it at the same time, giving you veining on leaves and petals, for example.

You must use only paper in these punches otherwise they will break. The embossing adds realism to the flowers and leaves. By lightly dabbing the shapes with an inkpad we highlight the embossing and make the flower and leaf colours look more natural at the same time.

In this project we punch flowers and leaves to create a hanging wreath. If you omit the ribbon, you can create a centrepiece for your dining table. Alternatively, just create two or three flowers for a really special card.

Your wreath will look lovely hanging on a window or door, over a fireplace or simply on the wall. Remember, though, that the flowers are made from paper – your wreath is not suitable for outdoor use. But it looks ideal on a front door inside an apartment block (as overleaf)!

Step by Step Instructions

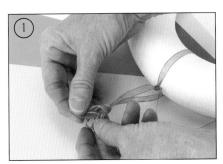

(1)

Take the 50cm length of ribbon, wrap around the wreath, tie a knot and then tie the two ends to create a hanging loop.

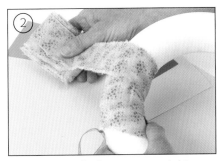

(2)

Glue one end of your material to the wreath and wrap, overlapping as you go until the whole wreath is covered. Secure the end with glue.

(3)

Punch eight flowers from pink paper and eight from blue paper. Dab or gently swipe the purple inkpad over the embossed centre of all the flowers.

(4)

Swipe the edges of the pink flowers with both a pink and a salmon coloured inkpad and the edges of blue flowers with a blue and an aquamarine inkpad.

(5)

Take four pink flowers and four blue flowers and cut away two of the petals at opposite sides to each other. Re-ink the bare edges.

(6)

Glue to the centre of the uncut flowers. When the glue is dry lift the cut flowers forward to create a 3D effect.

continued over

continued

Punch 16 stamen shapes from dark green paper. Colour the circles with black glaze pen. Glue two shapes to the centre of each flower. Pull the stamens forward.

Punch eight small circles from dark orange paper using the small hole punch and glue one to the centre of each flower.

Hints & Tips   Use three different shades of ink to make your flowers and leaves look realistic.

Punch 20 leaves from green paper. Highlight the embossing by sweeping a green, a brown and a dark green inkpad over the leaves.

Glue the flowers and leaves on the wreath. When the glue is dry tease the shapes into position with your finger.

Potted plant

Stretching paper or card will cause it to curve. Here we will curve punched floral shapes to create life-like flowers on wire stems.

By securing them in clay in a plant pot you'll create the ideal potted plant – one that is in flower all year long and doesn't need watering!

The card you use needs to be coloured on both sides as the plant is likely to be viewed from all angles. The colours of the flowers could of course be changed to suit your taste.

You will need:

- 7.5cm daisy punch
- 5cm daisy punch
- 3.5cm daisy punch
- 2.5cm stamen punch – sometimes known as a blink blink punch
- Several shades of thin yellow card
- Two shades of thin green card
- Thin dark brown card
- Light brown fluid chalk inkpad
- Orange Sakura glaze pen
- Embossing tool
- Embossing pad or mouse mat
- PVA glue
- Nut brown colour Flower Soft
- Small plastic plant pot
- 3D glue dots
- Heavy gauge green garden wire
- Wire cutters
- Air drying clay

To curve petals

Hold a daisy in one hand and a pair of closed scissors or similar underneath the shape with the other. Place the thumb of the hand the scissors are in on top of the petal so that you can feel the scissors below, and slowly and gently pull the scissors towards the edge of the petal. Repeat this several times – the action is similar to paring fruit or vegetables. By pulling the scissors along the underside of the paper you are stretching it and so it curves.

Step by Step Instructions

Punch 10 large daisies from light yellow card, 10 medium-size from mid-yellow card and 10 small daisies from the dark yellow card.

Ink around the edges of the petals. Just a little colour gives depth to the shapes.

Curve the petals. Curve the larger shapes slightly; more intensely on the smaller ones.

Put aside five of the large daisies. Layer and glue the rest to make five flowers. Each will have one large, two medium and two small daisy shapes.

Punch five stamen shapes from dark brown card. Colour the circles with orange glaze pen. Leave to dry thoroughly.

Place stamens on an embossing mat. Make gentle circular movements with an embossing tool in the centre of each to curve the ends of the stamens forward.

Hints & Tips Make sure your flowers face in different directions for a realistic look.

continued over

continued

Attach one to the centre of each flower. Add a little PVA glue and sprinkle with brown Flower Soft. When dry, shake off the excess.

Cut five 30cm lengths of green garden wire and attach to the front of the set aside daisies with a 3D glue dot. Secure a flower on top.

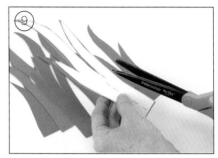

Use the templates (opposite) to cut leaves from two shades of green card. Fold along the dotted lines and curve a few as you did for the daisies.

Two-thirds fill a plant pot with air drying clay. Arrange the daisies in a bunch of varying heights. Cut the stems level and insert into the clay.

Push the leaves in around them and allow the clay to dry.

Once the clay has set, squeeze PVA glue on top of the clay and sprinkle with brown Flower Soft to give the impression of soil.

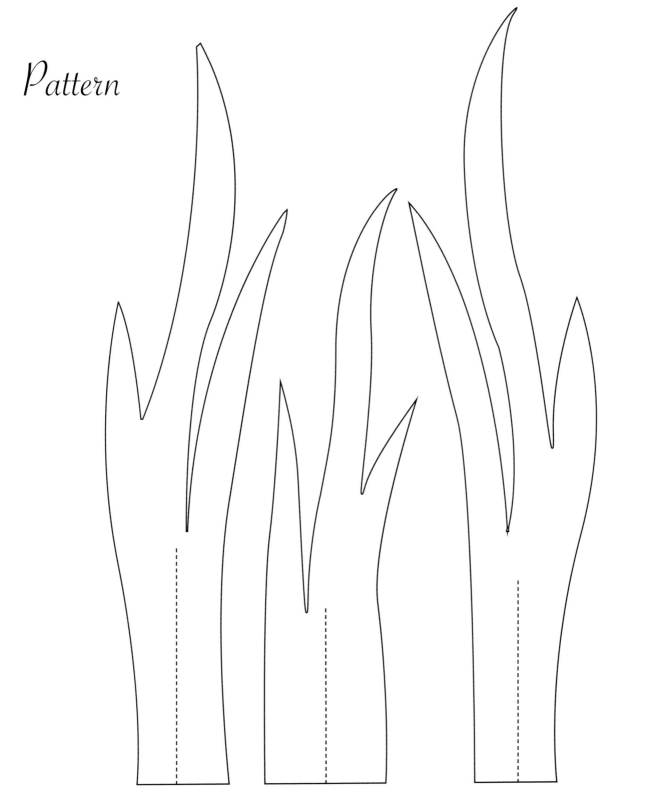

Pattern

Cherry blossom necklace

You can use two different punches over the same area of paper to create different shapes.

Here we'll use a small hole punch within a cherry blossom shape to make 'beads' to decorate a necklace. It doesn't matter whether you punch the cherry blossom or the hole first – try it both ways and see which suits you best!

Vilene is used in place of paper. It will go through a small paper punch readily, but is more durable than paper and so suitable for wearable art, such as this necklace. You should be able to buy it in any good curtain-making store.

Vilene can be coloured with any type of acrylic paint. We used one with a pearlescent finish to give a nice sheen to the beads, but ordinary acrylic paint would be fine. Don't feel you need to limit yourself to one colour either – multi-coloured flower beads would really make your necklace stand out from the crowd.

If you prefer, you can use ribbon instead of waxed cotton cord. Try making shorter versions of the necklace as matching bracelets or anklets. Alternatively, just make one flower bead and attach a brooch pin or use to decorate a hair clip.

You will need:

- 3.5cm cherry blossom punch
- Small hole punch
- Craft or pelmet Vilene
- Lumiere acrylic paint in pearlescent magenta or any acrylic paint
- Fourteen 12mm diameter pale pink buttons
- Five pink beads
- 1 metre waxed cotton cord
- Kitchen baking paper
- Household iron

Step by Step Instructions

Punch seven cherry blossom shapes from your pelmet Vilene. Punch a small hole in the centre.

Paint both sides of the shapes with acrylic paint and allow to dry.

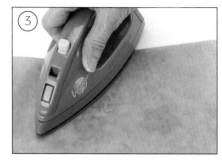

Place the shapes between two sheets of baking paper and dry iron for three minutes to heat set the paint.

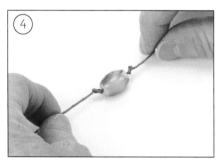

Thread a bead to the centre of your waxed cord and tie a knot at either side.

Pass the cord through a button, through the hole in the blossom, up through another button and down again, back through the blossom and then the first button.

The blossom will be held secure with a button on either side. Slide it into position approximately 2cm away from the bead.

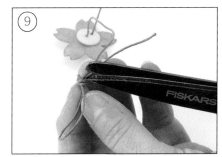

Leave 2cm of cord and secure another bead. Continue until you have three blossoms and two beads on either side of the central bead.

Leave approximately 12cm of cord on one side and then thread another cherry blossom. Knot the cord on the reverse and cut away the excess.

Leave the same distance on the other end. Create a loop large enough to just pass over the blossom and tie a knot. Trim away the excess.

Hints & Tips Remember to heat set your paint – you don't want it to stain your clothing.

Masculine leaves card

In this project we'll use both the punched shape as a template for embossing on metal shim and the negative of punched shapes as stencils to create a background for your card.

Metal shim is fine sheet metal that can be cut, pierced, punched and sewn. It's available from general purpose craft stores and is usually wrapped around cardboard tubing and sealed to keep in good condition. It's a good material to give a masculine look to a card.

If you're having difficulty finding metal shim, heavyweight kitchen foil or the inside of a tomato paste tube could be used instead.

Once the metal shim has been embossed or punched it may be quite wrinkled and uneven. Lay it on a firm flat surface and rub the back of your finger nail over it to smooth it flat again.

3D crystal lacquer gives a nice glazed finish to the embossed leaf, but you could colour it with permanent marker pens or alcohol inks instead if you prefer.

You will need:

- 18cm x 13cm cream card blank
- Green paper
- Brown paper
- Dark green card
- Cream card
- Scrap card or paper
- 3cm maple leaf punch
- 3cm fern punch
- 3cm leaf punch
- 1.5cm leaf punch
- Copper metal shim
- Mouse mat
- Embossing tool
- Green 3D crystal lacquer
- Fluid chalk inkpads in green, dark green and brown
- 12 small brown brads

Step by Step Instructions

①

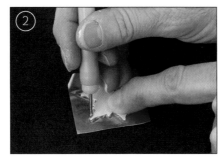

②

③

Punch a maple leaf from thin scrap card and place in the centre of a 4cm square of metal shim on a mouse mat.

Outline the maple leaf with the embossing tool using firm even pressure. When you take the card away you'll see the depressed outline of the leaf.

Turn the shim over so that the raised outline is uppermost and fill the area within the outline with green crystal lacquer. Set aside to dry.

④

⑤

⑥

Punch two maple leaves from the metal shim and mount each on a 4cm square of dark green card.

Mount each of the three leaf designs on a 4.5cm square of cream card and attach evenly down a 16cm x 5.5cm rectangle of brown paper.

Mount on a 17.5 x 7cm rectangle of green paper and place small brown brads in each of the corners of the squares.

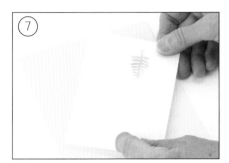

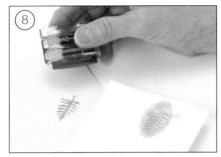

Hints & Tips Punched stencils could also be used with fabric paints to embellish a plain T-shirt.

Punch a fern from a scrap of paper. Discard the fern and place the scrap paper somewhere on the right-hand side of your card blank.

Rub an inkpad over the aperture, ensuring colour gets right into the edges of the shape. Remove the scrap paper to see the design inked on your card.

Repeat the process using all three leaf shapes randomly over the right-hand side of the card. Vary the ink colour as you go.

Mount the maple leaf design to the left-hand edge of the card.

Scrapbook-style wall-mounted picture

In this project we will combine some of the techniques we have learned to create a scrapbook-style picture on an artist's canvas block. It hangs on the wall or stands on a shelf.

The techniques that you need to have tried are: making patterns (page 25), decorating shapes (page 28), using a border punch to create faux lace (page 40) and punching within a punch (page 62).

We chose red for the tag as it complements the colour of the sweatshirt in the photo, and black for the hearts to go with the background paper. You may wish to vary the colours of paper and card used to co-ordinate with your chosen photograph.

The same ideas could of course be used on a normal scrapbook page, greetings card or the lid of a stationery box.

You will need:

- 20cm x 20cm canvas block
- Black acrylic paint
- Patterned black paper
- Thin black, red and silver card
- White paper
- Heirloom hearts punch
- 4.5cm tag punch
- Hearts border punch
- 2.5cm heart punch
- 1.5cm heart punch
- 1cm heart punch
- Small hole punch
- Silver heart-shaped brad
- Small crystal adhesive gems

Step by Step Instructions

Paint your canvas block. You don't need to paint right into the centre as it will be covered by the paper.

Cut a 19.5cm square of patterned black paper. Cut a 1cm strip of thin black card and attach 2cm from the base.

Create some paper lace by punching both sides of a 4cm wide strip of white paper with the border punch.

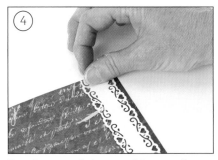

Retain two of the small hearts from the punch as waste. Attach the lace vertically close to the right-hand edge of the paper.

Attach your photo.

Punch the three heirloom hearts twice from black card. Attach the largest hearts to the top right- and bottom left-hand corners of your photo.

Hints & Tips Change the paint colour to match your decor

Attach two of the smaller hearts in a suitable place over your photo. Keep the remaining two smaller hearts for another project.

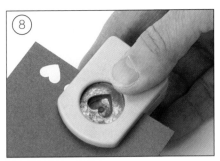

Punch three 1cm hearts in a row on thin red card.

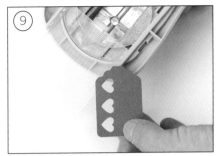

Place the tag punch upside down over the heart apertures and punch the tag so that the hearts appear down one side.

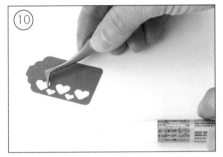

Attach two of the small hearts from the border punch waste to the side of the tag.

Punch a 1.5cm heart from black card. Place the 2.5cm heart punch upside down over the heart-shaped space just created and punch again.

Attach the created heart frame and a brad to the tag. Attach the tag near the base of the photo with 3D foam tape.

Punch four red and two silver 1cm hearts. Punch two silver small circles. Use to create a pattern along the black strip either side of the tag.

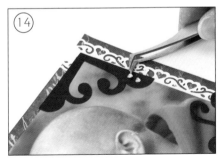

Add some small crystal gems to the largest punched hearts and to the pattern strip.

Attach the completed design to your canvas block.

3D floral greetings card

This is an intricate, high relief greetings card, combining some techniques learned earlier. The ones you'll need to have tried are: corner punching (page 22), creating 3D flowers (page 53) and using a punched shape as a stencil (page 67).

We've used chalks to create the background and colour flowers and leaves, but you could use inkpads instead.

You could give the card a more masculine look by using autumn leaves instead of flowers and by making the design more linear.

3D flowers could be used instead of a bow when wrapping a parcel or tied around the neck of a bottle when presenting it to your dinner host.

You will need:

- 20cm x 15cm cream card blank
- Blue card
- Cream card
- Blue double-sided paper
- Green double-sided paper
- Small pieces of cream, blue, pink and lilac paper
- Ornate corner punch
- Embossing flower punch
- Embossing oak leaf punch
- 2.5cm stamen punch – sometimes known as a blink blink punch
- Small flowers multi punch or several individual small flower punches
- 1cm maple leaf punch
- Embossing tool
- Embossing mat
- Decorating craft chalks
- Blue glitter
- Black Sakura glaze pen
- Fine point pens
- Double-sided tape
- 3D foam tape

Step by Step Instructions

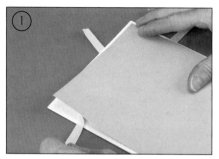

1. Cut a 19cm x 14cm rectangle of blue card and attach to the front of the card blank.

2. Cut an 18cm x 13cm rectangle of cream card and punch the corners with the decorative corner punch.

3. Place double-sided tape on the reverse of the punched corners. Don't remove the backing.

4. Sprinkle glitter over the sticky side of the tape showing through the punched areas. Press it onto the tape with your finger. Shake off the excess.

5. Punch the small maple leaf onto scrap card. Use as a stencil with decorative chalks to create a leaf pattern over the cream card. Attach to the base card.

6. Punch four large flowers from blue paper and three large leaves from green. Use your decorating chalks to add realism to the flowers and leaves.

Hints & Tips
Protect your 3D flowers by placing this card in a box rather than an envelope.

Fold the edges of the petals forward. Create two flowers by layering the shapes with 3D foam tape.

Punch four stamens from cream paper, colour with black glaze pen and decorate the centres with small light brown and black dots.

Glue two sets of stamens together in double layers and attach to the centres of the flowers with 3D foam tape.

Attach the flowers and leaves to the card. Bend the leaves to make them look more realistic. Pull the top layer of stamens forward.

Punch several sets of small flowers from pink, blue and lilac paper and place them on an embossing mat.

Make gentle circular motions with the embossing tool in the centre of each flower and all the petals will gradually come forward.

Glue some flowers together in double layers and leave others single.

Add either single glaze pen dots or a group of fine pen dots to the centre of each flower.

Arrange them around the larger flowers on the card and glue in place.

Gardener's concertina notebook

I've created this simple, concertina-folding notebook as a gift for an avid gardener. There are little envelopes on the inside cover to store spare seeds and blank pages for writing notes.

You can adapt the notebook to any theme you wish – birthday dates, 'to do' lists or just a general jotter.

The decoration of the book covers combines several techniques that you used earlier, along with an alternative way of using corner punches. The techniques you need to have tried are: using the negative of a shape (page 33) and creating accurate borders (page 45).

You will need:

- Thick cardboard for creating book covers
- Patterned paper
- Thin green, blue, turquoise, yellow and brown card
- Decorative lever corner punch with removable paper guide – dart pattern
- 3.5cm circle punch
- 2cm plant pot punch
- 2.5cm daisy punch
- 1.5cm daisy punch
- 1cm flower punch
- Envelope punch (optional)
- Four 20cm lengths of ribbon
- Approx 10cm thin green wire
- Wire cutters
- Miniature buttons
- 3D glue dots
- 3D foam tape
- Wall lining paper for the pages

Step by Step Instructions

①

Cut two 15cm squares from cardboard and cover in patterned paper to create the covers for your book.

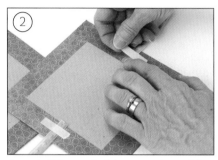

②

Attach 20cm of ribbon to the mid-point on both sides on the reverse of both covers. These are the closure ties for your book.

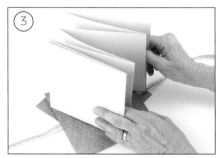

③

Cut a 14.5cm x 116cm long strip of lining paper. Fold the paper, concertina fashion, into 14.5cm squares.

④

Attach the first square to the inside of the front cover and the last square to the back cover.

⑤

Cut a 14cm x 5cm strip of thin yellow card. Mark the mid-point (7cm) and a point 4.5cm to the right and left of the mid-point.

⑥

Remove the paper guide from the back of your corner punch and hold the punch upside down.

Hints & Tips Using wall lining paper for the pages means you avoid having any joins.

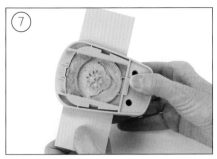

Align a marked point on your card with the centre of the punch design and punch.

Repeat for the other marked points. Retain some of the small shapes that fall as waste from the punch.

Cut a 14cm x 12cm rectangle of green card and slide the right-hand edge under the decorative pattern made by the corner punch.

Attach both pieces to a 14.5cm square of blue card. Complete the border with miniature buttons.

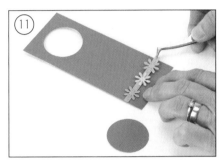

Punch a circle in the top of a 13cm x 5.5cm rectangle of turquoise card. Decorate the base with small daisies on a strip of card.

Attach with 3D foam tape. Punch two 2.5cm yellow daisies. Add small punched flower and button centres. Add wire stems and attach to the aperture with glue dots.

Punch two flower pots from brown card. Attach one over the wire stems. Cut the rim from the second and attach with 3D foam tape.

Cut a narrow blue strip of card to fit the design and decorate with the retained waste shapes from the corner punch. Attach to book front.

You may wish to create a decorative panel for the inside cover of your book and attach three punched and folded miniature envelopes.

Index

3D crystal laquer	67
3D floral card	75
Accurate borders	45
Bookmark	25
Border punches	10, 40, 70
Button punches	10, 15
Cards (greetings)	17, 19, 22, 33, 75
Chalking	75
Concertina folding	78
Corner punches	10, 22, 48, 75, 78
Crystal lacquer	67
Curving	57
Decorating shapes	28
Emboss punches	10, 53, 75
Embossing on metal	67
Faux lace	40, 70
Floral wreath	53
Gift card	22
Inking	53
Leaves (card)	67
Lever punches	10, 15
Long arm punches	10

Making patterns	25
Metal shim	67
Necklace	62
Negative of a shape	33
Notebook	78
Notebook cover	45
Photo frames	37
Pillow box	28
Plier punches	10
Potted plant	57
Punch aid	10
Punch care	12
Punched shapes as stencil	67
Punched waste	22, 36
Punching within a punch	62, 70
Scrapbook style	70
Stencil	67
Stretching (paper/card)	57
Squeeze punches	10, 48
Table decorations	48
Templates	32, 61
Three dimensional shapes	48
Trinket box	40
Veining	53
Vilene	62
Wallmounting	70